# Walk In Your
# AUTHORITY

Other Books by Allison Gregory Daniels

*Life Goes On: How to Maintain Your Faith Through Adversity*
*Taking Back My Life: A Collection of Inspirational Thoughts*
*Facing Tomorrow: A Collection of Short Stories*

# Walk In Your AUTHORITY
### Unleashing the Divine Power From Within

## ALLISON GREGORY DANIELS

**WALK IN YOUR AUTHORITY**
Published by Purposely Created Publishing Group™

Copyright © 2016 Allison Gregory Daniels

ALL RIGHTS RESERVED.

No part of this book may be reproduced, distributed or transmitted in any form by any means, graphics, electronics, or mechanical, including photocopy, recording, taping, or by any information storage or retrieval system, without permission in writing from the publisher, except in the case of reprints in the context of reviews, quotes, or references.

Unless otherwise indicated, scripture quotations are from the King James Version®. Copyright © 1982 by Thomas Nelson, Inc. All rights reserved.

Printed in the United States of America

ISBN (ebook): 13: 978-1-942838-91-3
ISBN (paperback): 13: 978-1-942838-90-6

---

Special discounts are available on bulk quantity purchases by book clubs, associations and special interest groups. For details email: sales@publishyourgift.com or call (888) 949-6228.

*For information logon to:*
www.PublishYourGift.com

# Acknowledgments

I extend my sincere gratitude to…

— My Lord my God from whom all blessings flow

— My soul mate Earl, for all his love and support

— My precious daughters, Kristian and Damona: I love you both so much and I am very proud of you both

— My mom and my dad (Cha Cha), who have believed in me from the very start

— My Pastors Daniel and Sabrina Mangrum, who impart the true Word of God they preach and teach to their congregation, as well as walk in a right-standing manner with integrity

— Both my sister and my brother: keep on believing in God and delighting in Him, because God will give you the desires of your heart as you continue to trust in Him

— Family and friends for their support. There are too many of you to name, but you all know who you are and I thank you again and again.

# Words of Encouragement

May God's Grace continue to be with you! My heart is so excited about what God has in store for each of you and for me. To God, I give all glory, honor, and praise for the words He has placed into my hands to write my thirty-first book.

I pray that you will open up your heart and receive what God has to say to you. Whatever you might be going through now, you must trust Him and know that He is speaking directly to you in areas that require deliverance. There is a word in due season in this book for you, because God's loving hand has directed my heart, mind, and spirit. I pray that this book will strengthen your heart so that you may find a greater love from my Heavenly Father as you walk out your spiritual journey. I encourage you to read and meditate on God's Word daily to gain a closer walk with Him.

This book is about a journey to wholeness and self-awareness of the God in you. He has set you apart and predestined you to become conformed to the image of His Son. God wants you to know that even in your uncertain seasons you have to live through, laugh through, and love through to move forward. So, rise up, walk in your authority, and make a stand as God moves you to your next level.

# Table of Contents

Acknowledgments ........................................................................... v

Words of Encouragement............................................................. vi

Chapter 1  Walk in Your Authority ............................................13

Chapter 2  Pursue Your Purpose.................................................21

Chapter 3  Standing in the Midst of a Storm.........................25

Chapter 4  The Female Architect: Your Personal Blueprint to Building Confidence ...............................................35

Chapter 5  Breaking the Cycle ....................................................41

Chapter 6  Bully Me No More—Move On................................44

Chapter 7  Embracing Change and Personal Transition....................................................................49

Chapter 8  Create Your Own Destiny Now ..............................57

Chapter 9  Take Charge..................................................................61

Prayer of Salvation .........................................................................65

About the Author............................................................................67

## BRIEF SYNOPSIS OF THE BOOK

You can maintain your life after the storm and walk in your authority, and you can know and unleash the divine power from within.

In this book, *Walk in Your Authority: Unleashing the Divine Power from Within*, author Allison Gregory Daniels shares how she weathered the storms of life by taking you through her life experiences and showing you how she stood trusting God in the midst of it all. Her refusal to allow life's events to destroy God's plan and her saved her and solidified her identity. This book is a step-by-step guide, offering powerful tips, strategies, and tools for overcoming your passed hurts, surviving emotional setbacks, and handling your emotions. Daniels offers testimony to the faith and trust she placed in God, as well as the reassurance that past experiences do not have to destroy future dreams. She knew that she would stand, live, love, and laugh again, once she changed her thinking and dealt with her past disappointments, which then reconnected her to her journey of wholeness.

By walking in your authority and unleashing the divine power from within, you will be challenged and encouraged to believe that, no matter what you're going through, you must trust God and know that He is speaking directly to you in areas you need change. So trust that He is preparing, positioning and elevating you to your next level. Even in your seasons of uncertainty, loss, and lack, He is still worthy of praise.

## Chapter 1:

## **WALK IN YOUR AUTHORITY**

*"Every place that the sole of your foot shall tread upon, that have I given unto you, as I said unto Moses."*

**Joshua 1:3**

I remember back in 1983, I had a dream in which I saw myself walking up a steep hill in a long white robe with a Bible in my hand, preaching to a multitude of people. Back then, I had no idea that I was walking in my calling. I knew that God was top priority in my life and that I had to go through a process to see the plans that He had for my life but I was at a loss for words then.

One day, I prayed to God for a title for my new book and He said, "Walk in your authority." Walk in your authority! As a minister, that's all I kept hearing God say, His words constantly ringing in my ear.

"Walk in your authority! Step out on your faith and believe that I, your Lord and your God, called you and not man."

So, I wrote down several things that I felt God was calling me to do. Below, you can write down your vision or goals for your own life.

## *YOUR VISION/YOUR GOALS*

*"And the* Lord *answered me, and said, Write the vision, and make it plain upon tables, that he may run that readeth it."*

**Habakkuk 2:2**

Goal 1: _____
Goal 2: _____
Goal 3: _____

You need courage to fulfill the assignments and plans that He has for your life, and you must learn how to walk in the fruit of the spirit. Allow God to guide you to your truth. You must continue to wear the breastplate of righteousness and put on the full armor of God. You must continue to fight the good fight and walk in your authority.

## *THINGS YOU NEED TO DO WHILE WAITING ON GOD*

1. Make prayer a priority in your life.
2. Have a strong, committed, and intimate relationship with God.
3. Confess to God that you need His help and His guidance.
4. Live with the awareness of God's constant presence in your life.

*Make time to listen for God's voice by doing the following:*

1. Learn how to surrender your all to Him.
2. Anticipate that God is getting ready to please you.
3. Receive His great plan for your life.
4. Set aside time to be alone with God, to hear His voice, and expect Him to deliver you the answers to your prayers.

Constantly meditate on God's Word: *"Have not I commanded thee? Be strong and of a good courage; be not afraid, neither be thou dismayed: for the Lord thy God is with thee whithersoever thou goest"* (Joshua 1:9). And believe the same thing that Joshua believed when God said to Him, *"Every place that the sole of your foot shall tread upon, that have I given unto you, as I said unto Moses"* (Joshua 1:3), and *"There shall not any man be able to stand before thee all the days of thy life: as I was with Moses, so I will be with thee: I will not fail thee, nor forsake thee"* (Joshua 1:5).

## QUESTIONS TO ASK YOURSELF

1. How has God sustained me in the midst of my storms?

2. What does it mean to walk in my God-given authority?

3. What does it mean to walk in the unconditional love that God teaches?

4. Am I walking in faith or am I walking in fear?

Walk in your authority and in your God-given gift, the gift God has equipped you with. Make sure that you are determined, rooted, and grounded as you wait on the Lord. Be obedient to the call on your life and trust God to handle your issues. Remember, listening to the Lord is a vital part of your growth and development in His Word. So, as you walk in your authority, wait patiently on the Lord, trust in Him, believe in His favor, and believe in His Word: *"This I say then, Walk in the Spirit, and ye shall not fulfil the lust of the flesh"* (Galatians 5:16).

I encourage you to read a Bible verse daily and ask God to give you clear understanding of how His Word and principles pertain to your everyday life. Ask Him to grant you His wisdom in and out of season. Then, record your thoughts, insights, prayers, or poems in the "Walk in Your Authority" section of this book.

*Walk in Your Authority*

## Chapter 2:

## PURSUE YOUR PURPOSE

*"For I know the thoughts that I think toward you, saith the Lord, thoughts of peace, and not of evil, to give you an expected end."*

Jeremiah 29:11

Recently, my pastor conducted a bible study class on "Why Purpose is Important." Pastor Mangrum stated that purpose gives us content that we can fit into a meaningful framework, because (1) our purpose as Christians must drive our day-to-day and long-term decisions, (2) our purpose is to live for Christ and have Him live through us in constant interaction, and (3) our purpose mandates that we not engage in certain kinds of activities or practices.

So, each day you must get up and pursue the purpose for your life. You must believe in yourself that you can do whatever you set your mind to. The Word of God says, "I can do all things through Christ which strengthens me" (Philippians 4:13). It's time for you to have a survival mindset. The old mindset you used to have must be renewed, restored, and revitalized so that you will be ready for your next level. Make a choice to be happy, to begin again, to love, laugh, and dream again.

In order for you to get to your next level, you must recognize your strengths and embrace them. You have the ability to enlarge your vision and change the way you see things by allowing God to establish your thoughts. If you renew your mind on His Word, you will then become strengthened in Him and eventually be made new. The Word of God says, *"And be not conformed to this world: but be ye transformed by the renewing of your mind, that ye may prove what is that good, and acceptable, and perfect, will of God"* (Romans 12:2).

## *WAYS TO TRANSFORM YOUR MIND*

1. Choose to trust God first.
2. Meditate upon His Word every day.
3. Be determined to wait on the Lord for your answers.
4. Surrender your all to God.

## *QUESTIONS TO ASK YOURSELF*

1. How would my life change if I seek God for His answers early in the morning?

   _____

   _____

2. Am I mindful of God's presence in my life? If so, how and in what way?

   _____

   _____

3. Do I have a personal relationship with God? If so, how do I know?

   _____

   _____

As you grow, you will begin to recognize how God is slowly transforming your mind and healing your heart, all at the same time. So let the healing begin *with you* and start smiling through your tears—release what's causing you pain. Begin again. Believe me: it is okay for you to start all over again and re-evaluate your life. Live with confidence and move toward the next chapter in your life. You have the ability to see, visualize, and change what you see, hear, and speak out of *your* mouth.

## Chapter 3:

# STANDING IN THE MIDST OF A STORM

*"Wherefore take unto you the whole armour of God, that ye may be able to withstand in the evil day, and having done all, to stand."*

**Ephesians 6:13**

In early February of 2014, my mom told me that she wasn't feeling well and that she was going to face some challenges in her life. She said that she had some trying days ahead of her and that she was going to go on a journey, but she was not afraid or scared, because God had already told her that He would be with her and would never leave her.

Eventually, it was diagnosed that she needed to have thyroid surgery and underwent the procedure in May 2014. After the surgery, I noticed that she still was not quite herself, but I couldn't put my finger on it. She kept going back and forth to the doctors, because they couldn't seem to get her medicine right. For several months, my parents were in and out of the emergency room or visiting the doctors' offices. But what was strange to me was that she was constantly prescribed more medicine, in addition to the medications she was already taking. This went on for a few months. My mom would call me or one of my siblings to let us know that her doctors prescribed her some more medicine, but it all didn't add up. She kept saying, "It's okay, it's okay, I feel better." She didn't want us to worry about her.

On July 7, 2014, my whole life was turned upside down in a matter of minutes. It was about 2:30 in the morning. I kept hearing voices and loud noises. I just thought that it was my mom and dad getting up very early this particular morning, because we are all early risers. So, I went into my home office and started praying and reading my Bible, which is what I do every morning before I leave for work at 5:15 am. But this sound was different; the knocking started getting louder and louder. I ran down the stairs to see what was going on. It was my mom.

She kept saying, "I want to get out of here, I have to leave. I want to go home."

I said, "Mom what's wrong? What is going on?"

She had become very agitated while looking for her keys and said that my dad refused to give them to her. She hollered at me, "You call yourself a minister? You call yourself a child of God? Then stand your ground and find out what happened to me! Stand your ground, stand on your faith; stand on the Word of God, which you claim that you believe in. Hold your ground, hold your peace, preacher, and find out what happened to me."

I kept hearing this scripture in my head over and over again:

*"Finally, my brethren, be strong in the Lord, and in the power of his might. Put-on the whole armor of God, that ye may be able to stand against the wiles of the devil. For we wrestle not against flesh and blood, but against principalities, against powers, against the rulers of the darkness of this world, against spiritual wickedness in high places. Wherefore take unto you the whole armor of God, that ye may be able to withstand in the evil day, and having done all, to stand. Stand therefore, having your loins girt about with truth, and having on the breastplate of righteousness; And your feet shod with the preparation of the gospel of peace; Above all, taking the shield of faith, wherewith ye shall be able to quench all the fiery darts of the wicked. And take the helmet of salvation, and the sword of the Spirit, which is the word of God: Praying always with all prayer and supplication in the Spirit, and watching thereunto with all perseverance and supplication for all saints" (Ephesians 6:10-18)*

I had to call 911 and my mom was rushed to the hospital, because my mom kept trying to get out of the house. From this point on, in addition to the doctors' monitoring her and their prescribed treatments for her, I also kept track of everything. I immediately created a red notebook of every hospital and doctor's appointment my mom had from the day after her thyroid surgery. My dad and siblings were also right by my mom's side, reading over every piece of paper, medicine, and decision that was made on her behalf.

We all met with at least eleven doctors, several nurses and nurse assistances at the first hospital my mom was admitted to. The doctors asked if we wanted to have our mom undergo additional tests because they couldn't find anything wrong with her based on the initial tests. But instead of addressing us as a whole family, the doctors met with each of us, one by one, individually. My family and I were not in agreement to the individual discussions, because the common goal of our entire family was to find out what happened to our mother; so from that point on, the doctors began meeting with me, my dad, and my siblings, all together at once. If one of us was missing from the group, we would wait for that family member to return so that we could all be addressed to and informed at the same time.

If you have a loved one who might be going through an episode in his or her life, you need to stand your ground and band together so that you can get the answers you need and deserve. Do not allow someone to say, "We don't know what happen to your loved one" or "We don't have an answer for the family." Stand your ground and keep asking questions. Stay focused, calm, alert, but polite, and by all means, be firm.

As I contemplated what to do next, things in my mother's life and health began to spin out of control. Over a period of seven to eight months, my mom was admitted into seven different hospitals and we, as a family, saw over twenty-five doctors. But, the final straw came when I had to make a decision to take my mom off this roller coaster ride and put my foot down as her power-of-attorney. I had to make a decision (one which my family agreed with) to have my mother admitted into a short-term care nursing home until the doctors could figure out what went wrong. She had once been a healthy person who operated and functioned on her own; now, she didn't know who she was and why this had all happened to her at this time in her life.

It was difficult for us to place our loving mother and wife into the hands of strangers. When we visited the nursing home, she didn't want us to leave without taking her with us, but she was still not functioning at a point so we could leave her alone without hurting herself or someone else. Although my mom didn't know what was really going on, she knew how to call on the name of the Lord.

"Jesus, Jesus, I know that you are with me. Jesus, I know that you care about me," she would say over and over again. "Help my family find out what went wrong with me, because it has something to do with my medicine."

God is so awesome! He had many families, friends, church family, and co-workers praying and interceding for my mom, until the devil had to release her. After being in a nursing facility for just a short while, having several tests run, and visiting different specialists, they finally figured out what went wrong; my mom had had an allergic reaction to one of the medications that was given to her after her surgery, which hadn't agreed with the previous medications she was already taking. This particular medication interfered with her thought pattern and mechanical processes, as well as with her mobile abilities. Mentally and physically, it seemed as if my mom had gone from age sixty-eight to age two; both her mind and her body slowly regressed. Doctors didn't know what to do at the time, but then, another specialist came in and did an assessment on my mom, and prescribed her medication that reversed what she was going through. She slowly became herself again.

Ultimately, I know that we stood on the Word of God and, as a family, banded together and read and meditated on the scriptures below. These are just a few of the scriptures we stood on to focus on what God had planned for my mother:

*"Casting all your care upon him; for he careth for you."*

**1 Peter 5:7**

*"I waited patiently for the LORD; and he inclined unto me, and heard my cry. He brought me up also out of an horrible pit, out of the miry clay, and set my feet upon a rock, and established my goings. And he hath put a new song in my mouth, even praise unto our God: many shall see it, and fear, and shall trust in the Lord."*

**Psalms 40:1-3**

*"Let not your heart be troubled: ye believe in God, believe also in me. In my Father's house are many mansions: if it were not so, I would have told you. I go to prepare a place for you. And if I go and prepare a place for you, I will come again, and receive you unto myself; that where I am, there ye may be also."*

**John 14:1-3**

*"Fear thou not; for I am with thee: be not dismayed; for I am thy God: I will strengthen thee; yea, I will help thee; yea, I will uphold thee with the right hand of my righteousness."*

**Isaiah 41:10**

*"Be strong and of a good courage, fear not, nor be afraid of them: for the LORD thy God, he it is that doth go with thee; he will not fail thee, nor forsake thee."*

**Deuteronomy 31:6**

### *A Poem for my Mom*

*The hardest part of my life is letting my mom go.*

*The hardest part of my life is letting my mom go to strangers.*

*To place her in the arms of someone who doesn't share the love for her*

*That I have in my heart and mind for her.*

*The hardest part of my life is letting my mom go.*

*The hardest part of my life is letting her go and she never understands why,*

*As my heart breaks and cries from within and also on the outside,*

*The hardest part of my life is letting her go.*

*I've learned to trust God more and more.*

## *A Prayer for my Mom*

*O Merciful God, because of Your Word, my mom*
*Is an overcomer. She overcomes the world, the flesh and*
*the devil, by the Blood of the Lamb and the word of*
*her testimony. (1 John 4:4, Revelation 12:11)*

## Chapter 4:

# THE FEMALE ARCHITECT: YOUR PERSONAL BLUE PRINT TO BUILDING YOUR CONFIDENCE

*"For the Lord shall be thy confidence, and shall keep thy foot from being taken."*

**Proverbs 3:26**

What is confidence? Confidence is a belief or conviction that an outcome will be favorable or a solution will be found to a problem. Confidence is also generally described as a state of being certain whether about a hypotheses or prediction being correct or that a chosen course of action is the best or most effective.

*"For I know the thoughts that I think toward you, saith the LORD, thoughts of peace, and not of evil, to give you an expected end."*

**Jeremiah 29:11**

In order to start building your confidence up to the level that you want it to be, you must start by having a relationship with God who gives you the confidence to succeed in life.

## STEPS ON HOW TO BUILD YOUR CONFIDENCE

1. Schedule a set time just for you and God alone.
2. Step away from negative thinking.
3. Focus on positive things.
4. Speak up for yourself.
5. Change your body language.
6. Maintain a positive support network.
7. Enlarge your vision.

## THE POWER OF AFFIRMATION

Begin speaking life-changing words into your life. Below, you can make a list of your daily affirmations.

I am_____

I am_____

I am_____

# *CREATE YOUR OWN BLUEPRINT*

Blueprint# 1: What are my goals?

1. _____

2. _____

3. _____



Blueprint# 2: What are three things I want to pursue?

1. _____

2. _____

3. _____

## *WRITE YOUR PERSONAL THOUGHTS HERE*

---
---
---
---
---
---

## *STEPS TO START YOUR OWN DESTINY CHANGE*

1. Start thinking about where you want to go from here.
2. Take control of your own time.
3. Allow yourself to say, "No!"
4. Determine what is valuable to you.
5. Ask yourself what can you learn from your current situation.
6. Ask God to show you how to make a difference.
7. Create a vision of yourself being at peace after the healing process.

# *ENLARGE YOUR VISION PROCESSING CHART*

**From the OLD WAY OF THINKING    To A NEW WAY OF THINKING**

| | |
|---|---|
| Negative thoughts | Positive thoughts |
| Negative speaking | Positive speaking |
| Things will never change | Change is good |
| No one loves me | I am loved and highly favored |
| I am not a victim | I am a victor |
| I am not defeated | I am a survivor |
| I am not hated | I am loved |
| I am no longer sad | I have joy |
| I am hurt | I am healed |

## *KEEP A JOURNAL*

As a Life Coach, I encourage women and teens to remember that, no matter what they're going through, life goes on. You must begin to empower yourself and stop waiting for others to validate you. You are already of value to God. I encourage you to stop looking back at your past and move forward into your future. Stop letting the small things change your destiny. Stop allowing what others say about you and to you to define who you are. I encourage each person to keep a daily journal, which can help you release some of your daily anxieties and disappointments, while also confirming your achievements and goals.

Remember: writing in your journal each day gives you an opportunity to share your private thoughts and emotions, while revisiting your accomplishments; I am constantly writing in my journal, and I do so on a daily basis.

# Chapter 5:

## **BREAKING THE CYCLE**

*"A time to kill, and a time to heal; a time to break down, and a time to build up."*

**Ecclesiastes 3:3**

I had to tear Allison down. I had to break the cycle I was constantly in and delete and forget all of the things I had learned from age ten to thirty-five. I had to forget the things that were behind me and reach for the things before me. I had to persevere in going forward but only in God.

*"Brethren, I count not myself to have apprehended: but this one thing I do, forgetting those things which are behind, and reaching forth unto those things which are before, I press toward the mark for the prize of the high calling of God in Christ Jesus."*

**Philippians 3:13-14**

I decided that I wanted to leave behind people with negative thinking and speaking, so that I could open my mind to positive things that reflected my spiritual growth and to walk in the fruits of the Spirit: "*But the fruit of the Spirit is love, joy, peace, longsuffering, gentleness, goodness, faith*" (Galatians 5:22).

I knew that this was what God wanted me to do. I had to remove me from myself, and I had to stop running to others instead of running to God. Only He could solve Allison's problems. Only God could change this cycle I was on year after year, month after month, week after week, day after day, hour after hour, minute after minute. I had to decrease and allow the Spirit of God to increase. I had to stop living for Allison; my life was now God's.

I had to cut some people out of my life. There are some things that only God can speak to you about that others will not understand. There are some people, family, friends, and co-workers who will not believe that God has spoken to you, because they themselves don't want to go anywhere and they don't want you to go anywhere either.

I had to learn how to lean, trust, and depend on God. I recognized that I was in a growing period in my life and that I needed to be guided. I shuddered to think what my daughter would be like if I wasn't around to see her grow up. I thought I had to make up for lost times, but my time was in God's hand. I just needed to accept all that came with His life, death, and resurrection. I finally felt that shaking in my spirit; I finally felt a release of God's power over my life. The ropes and chains that had once entangled me had finally began releasing me.

Breaking the cycle of my life has been good to me through the years. God saved me through His Son, Jesus Christ: "*I can do all things through Christ which strengtheneth me*" (Philippians 4:13). But some of the emotions that rose up within me were shame, guilt, depression, anger, and fear. As we walk in *and* with God, we must remember not to allow our emotions to rule us.

## *QUESTIONS TO ASK YOURSELF*

1. What am I holding on to that's not good for me?

_____

_____

2. Have I discovered the person God wants me to be?

_____

_____

## Chapter 6:

## BULLY ME NO MORE—MOVE ON

*"For God hath not given us the spirit of fear; but of power, and of love, and of a sound mind."*

2 Timothy 1:7

What is bullying? Webster Dictionary describes it as aggressive, repeated actions such as taunting, threatening, hitting, harassing, intimidating, or otherwise harming another individual, giving the bully power over another person.

I recall telling my youngest daughter, who was eight-years-old at the time, on how to move on from bullying. I remember she never wanted to go to school or would make excuses for not wanting to go outside. I told her that bullying was wrong and she had to learn how to stand up for herself with confidence. As a parent, you must choose your words wisely, because this is a growing experience in which a child really doesn't understand why someone is being mean to them or why someone doesn't like them. But I believe in combating bullying by bringing awareness and helping people, especially victims of bullying: we must learn how to communicate with others about this serious problem, especially in our schools. Or else, bullying will get out of control, and both children and adults will start living in fear.

What resulted from my daughter's experience was my daughter's first book at age nine: *Bully Me No More*. We both grew together in building levels of self-esteem, confidence, and determination, and decided to help others see that communication is key to making a difference in one's life. If you are being bullied, whether you are an adult or a child, it's time to (1) reclaim your identity, (2) learn how to become your own best friend, (3) live life with a purpose, (4) learn to love and accept yourself, (5) eliminate poisonous relationships, (6) stop self-sabotage through negative behavior, and (7) learn from your past failures and challenges to move on. It's time for you to think outside the box and celebrate your own accomplishments, large or small. You deserve to be happy and free.

Each day, I hope that all children will learn how to get along with one another, communicate with each other, make quality relationships, be more caring, and speak up for themselves.

## *7 STEPS TO DEVELOPING YOUR SELF-ESTEEM*

1. Develop self-love first.
2. Develop confidence.
3. Speak life-changing words.
4. Change your mindset to think positive.
5. Overcome any guilt or shame.
6. Overcome negative thinking.
7. Develop daily affirmation techniques.

## *I PLEDGE…*

I pledge to help others.

I pledge to make a difference.

I pledge to report bullying.

I pledge to _____

_____

_____

# GREAT LEADERS LEAD IN A TIME OF CHANGE

## *QUESTION TO ASK YOURSELF*

Am I a leader or a follower?

*My answer:*

## *WRITE A LIST EVERYDAY ABOUT YOUR HAPPY TIMES*

## Chapter 7:

# EMBRACING CHANGE AND PERSONAL TRANSITION

*"To every thing there is a season, and a time to every purpose under the heaven:*

*A time to weep, and a time to laugh; a time to mourn, and a time to dance;*

*A time to cast away stones, and a time to gather stones together; a time to embrace, and a time to refrain from embracing;*

*A time to get, and a time to lose; a time to keep, and a time to cast away;*

*A time to rend, and a time to sew; a time to keep silence, and a time to speak;"*

**Ecclesiastes 3:1,4-7**

Falling in love with my husband was easy, but then came the questions of children. I already had one child, but in beginning my new life with my husband, I made the big decision to have my second child at the age of forty. With my first child, I was a single mother at twenty-five and, although I felt that I was too young to have a child, things were different back then. I had the patience to run from place to place when she had doctor's appointments; I had the time to spend on homework and school events; I had the strength to travel from place to place and not get so tired at one time.

With my second child, it was a challenge because my body was starting to change. My hormones were starting to set in and I was settling down within my spirit. So, when I found out that I was pregnant, my husband and I hit some roadblocks. Doctors told me that I was too old to have a child. I had to take several tests to ensure that my baby was not going to be disabled or in danger, but we believed in God and knew that He wouldn't send us an imperfect gift, no matter the baby's condition. I knew in my heart and mind that she (we learned the sex early on) was going to be okay, no matter what the doctors had to say. We trusted in the Word of God.

However, by this time, I felt that I was in between two worlds: I had one child who was getting ready to graduate from high school and another child that I needed to nurture and embrace to that next level. I had to adjust my attitude and change my way of thinking, because my patience had been worn thin and I had forgotten about everything that I learned in raising my first child. Still, having another baby had no place in my life until I met the man who I married and loved more than life itself; I wanted us both to share in the joy of seeing our child come to life and grow in God's abundance..

I had to learn to embrace the changes that I was getting ready to go through. Even with all of the challenges and uncertainties I had to encounter, transitional changes became an inevitable part of life. Embracing them made me stronger and wiser since I was able to grow and develop in the areas where I was weakest.

## *TEN POINTS TO PONDER*

1. Step out of your comfort zone and live.

2. Live, love, and laugh more each day.

3. Enlarge your visions, dreams, and desires.

4. Change your perspective on how you see things.

5. Create a balance in your life and live stress-free.

6. Center yourself around positive people who care about you and who will celebrate you.

7. Be quick to adapt to new changes.

8. Speak positive words about yourself to yourself each day.

9. Break down the strongholds that are keeping you bound.

10. Let go of the negative and allow God's Word to heal you.

I believe God gives us new strength: *"But they that wait upon the LORD shall renew their strength; they shall mount up with wings as eagles; they shall run, and not be weary; and they shall walk, and not faint"* (Isaiah 40:31). Each day, trust God to renew your heart and mind. The Bible says, *"And he changeth the times and the seasons: he removeth kings, and setteth up kings: he giveth wisdom unto the wise, and knowledge to them that know understanding"* (Daniel 2:21).

## *TRANSFORMATION SCRIPTURES*

*"Remember ye not the former things, neither consider the things of old. Behold, I will do a new thing; now it shall spring forth; shall ye not know it? I will even make a way in the wilderness, and rivers in the desert."*

**Isaiah 43:18-21**

*"And be renewed in the spirit of your mind;"*

**Ephesians 4:23**

*"...I am the light of the world: he that followeth me shall not walk in darkness, but shall have the light of life."*

**John 8:12**

*"Wait on the Lord: be of good courage, and he shall strengthen thine heart: wait, I say, on the Lord."*

**Psalms 27:14**

## *CREATE YOUR PERSONAL AFFIRMATIONS*

Today, I believe in change for the better. I believe that, when I pray, my prayers are answered.

Today, I plan to believe in the best for my life and _____

Today, I want to see change come into my new life.

Today, I give myself a way to change by _____.

Today, I will commit to reading a Bible verse every day.

Today, I will commit to pampering myself at least once a month.

## *Questions to Ask Yourself*

1. In the past, was there ever an obstacle in which God intervened on my behalf?

2. What are some of my strengths that I know keeps me going each day?

3. Do I have daily devotions that I start my days off with? If not, why?

4. What areas in my life need to be lined up with God so that He may take me to the next level?

5. Am I a victim or a survivor? Why?

## Chapter 8:

## CREATE YOUR OWN DESTINY NOW

*"For God hath not given us the spirit of fear; but of power, and of love, and of a sound mind."*

2 Timothy 1:7

It's time for you to create your own destiny. When you change your perception, you make a difference in your future. How you feel on the inside about yourself is going to determine how you view things on the outside. You have the power within you to change the course of your life. If you know within your heart that you are traveling in the wrong direction, make a U-turn. Take control of your destiny now and what you focus on most will give life to that destiny. Once you realize how important your destiny is to you, you will walk a new walk and talk a new talk.

Your future depends on *you*—it's time for you to put your life in perspective.

Each day, I challenge you to take inventory of yourself. Why? Because life-changing situations such as the loss of a loved one or job, battling low self-esteem, or getting hurt by someone we trust all play vital parts in how we process information and ultimately change our outlooks on certain situations. How much value you place on what happened to you will determine whether you can change your negative situation into a positive one.

## *THINK POSITIVE…*

I can make a difference.

I will succeed in life.

I can handle this situation that is placed before me.

I will not fail—I will prevail.

I am able to advance to the next level in my life.

# *WALK IN YOUR AUTHORITY:*
# *IT'S A LIFE PROCESS*

| *If ...* | *Scriptures to read...* |
|---|---|
| You are worried | Matthew 8:19-34 |
| You are losing hope | Psalm 126 |
| You are fearful | Psalm 3:7 |
| You need reassurance | Psalm 145:18 |
| You are sad | John 14 |
| You need security | Psalm 121:3 |
| You need courage | Joshua 1 |
| You need peace | Matthew 11:25-30 |

## Chapter 9:

## TAKE CHARGE

*"Be of good courage, and he shall strengthen your heart, all ye that hope in the Lord."*

**Psalm 31:24**

Take charge of your life NOW! This is a new day for you to take back your life and begin to live again. It's time for you to eliminate the self-defeating beliefs that you have about yourself. It's time for you to embrace who you are, take control of your emotions, and stop feeling inferior to others. Each and every day, learn how to forgive and accept yourself—enjoy your journey!

Release the things that are hindering you from moving to your next level. Sometimes the enemy will use people, situations, and or life's issues to distract you, to get you off focus, setting you up for any hurt, bitterness, shame, or blame. The Word of God says, *"Be not conformed to this world: but be ye transformed by the renewing of your mind, that ye may prove what is that good, and acceptable, and perfect, will of God"* (Romans 12:2).

Each day, you must enlarge your vision, because life goes on. If you have been hurt and disappointed, if you've lost a loved one or a dear friendship, life still goes on. The old mindset you used to have must be renewed, restored, and revitalized for your next level. Enlarging your vision means to think outside the box and come out of your comfort zone, so that you may break barriers of defeat, condemnation, and disappointment. Life goes on and you have to change how you deal with your disappointments to find your true path.

## WRITE DOWN THREE THINGS YOU CAN DO NOW TO ENLARGE YOUR VISION

1. _____

2. _____

3. _____

## *MOTIVATE YOURSELF*

I believe in myself and in the power of prayer, and I believe that I will achieve the plans and gifts that God has for my life. I surrender everything that I have to God and entrust Him to direct my path. I will learn how to be sensitive to the leading and guiding of the Holy Spirit, so that I can hear God's voice as He speaks to me. I pledge to spend more quality time with God each day.

The Word of God warns us that the enemy wants to steal from, kill, and destroy us, but God's Word says Jesus came to give life. If you let Jesus into your life, you can live life more abundantly with His love and guidance. As you enlarge your vision, remember that, although challenges will come, you must look closely inside your own heart for changes that will make a difference. The answers have always been within you and the time has come to take back your life. Change how you think about yourself and how God fits into your everyday life.

Take time out of each day to remind yourself that *you* matter and that you don't have to be perfect; instead, be persistent in achieving your goals. Remind yourself that you are going to carry out the plans for your future; you are going to complete each assignment that has been placed upon you and add happiness and value to your life. It's time for you to empower and encourage yourself, building your self-esteem and giving your life passion again. You have already survived your past hurts, overcome your emotional setbacks, and handled your roller coaster emotions. Now, create your own destiny and live again. Why? Because life goes on and you must, too.

As the Lord says, *"Seek ye first the kingdom of God, and his righteousness; and all these things shall be added unto you"* (Matthew 6:33). We must continue to seek God and strive to understand and recognize His character and love for us. Our faith must be based on the Word of God and not on our emotions for, when we learn how to seek God's will for our lives, He will unleash our God-given gifts to us. His Word states, *"In all thy ways acknowledge him, and he shall direct thy paths"* (Proverbs 3:6). Also, the Book of Proverbs deems, *"The righteousness of the perfect shall direct his way: but the wicked shall fall by his own wickedness"* (11:5).

When you seek God's will to unleash your creativity and transform your thinking into the plan He has created for your life and future, several things will begin to happen. You will begin to (1) sharpen your spirit and gain a clear direction for your life, (2) increase your faith and awareness of His power and presence, and (3) increase your ability to feel God's love operating as you move forward.

The world awaits your arrival. Your success lies in the fact that you know within yourself that a new season is blooming in your life and you're ready to move forward. Face your fears and hurts and celebrate yourself, building a bridge of hope. You are a living miracle and now you're free: no more hurt, no more pain, and no more sorrow. Come out of your comfort zone, rise above your circumstances, and look beyond your disappointments, because God is able.

## *PRAYER OF SALVATION*

Dear Heavenly Father,

I come to you now, asking for Your forgiveness. I am a sinner and I repent now. I make the decision right now to forsake my own will and turn away from my sins and turn to You. Your Word says, *"That if thou shalt confess with thy mouth the Lord Jesus, and shalt believe in thine heart that God hath raised him from the dead, thou shalt be saved"* (Romans 10:9).

I confess this now and I believe with my whole heart. I submit my life to You. Thank You for saving me and giving me Your Holy Spirit, who will now live in me and help me to obey You and live by Your Word.

*Pray this now, and always end in –Jesus' Name. Amen.*

# About the Author

Rev. Allison G. Daniels is a speaker, author, and the President & CEO of Allison Daniels Ministries, LLC. She conducts workshops and seminars that have been presented throughout the United States. The workshops and seminars conducted by the institute consist of topics such as: women in management, women as leaders, the Superwoman Syndrome, leadership skills, the assertive woman, customer service, and diversity and emotional wellness for women. In addition to leading these transformative experiences, Rev. Daniels has also been certified by the Professional Woman Network (PWN) as a professional coach and diversity consultant.

Rev. Daniels currently resides in Upper Marlboro, Maryland, with her husband, Earl, and their two daughters, Kristian and Damona.

## WE WANT TO HEAR FROM YOU!!!

If this book has made a difference in your life Rev. Allison would be delighted to hear about it.

**Leave a review on Amazon.com!**

---

**BOOK REV. ALLSION TO SPEAK AT YOUR NEXT EVENT!**

Send an email to: booking@publishyourgift.com

**FOLLOW REV. ALLSION ON SOCIAL MEDIA**

AllisonG.Daniels          AllisonDaniels9

---

"EMPOWERING YOU TO IMPACT GENERATIONS"

**WWW.PUBLISHYOURGIFT.COM**

**SEMINARS AND TOPICS OFFERED:**

Leadership Development

Career Development

Diversity

Survival Skills for Women and Youth

Business Development

**BOOKS BY ALLISON GREGORY DANIELS:**

*Life Goes On: How to Maintain Your Faith Through Adversity*

*Taking Back My Life: A Collection of Inspirational Thoughts*

*Facing Tomorrow: A Collection of Short Stories*

**OTHER BOOKS CO-AUTHORED:**

*Bully Me No More*

*Broken Peace*

*Teenage Girls: Guide for Health, Wellness and Self-Esteem*

*The Female Leader: Empowerment, Confidence & Passion*

*Celebration of Life: Inspiration for Women*

*Releasing Strongholds: Letting Go of What's Holding You Back*

*How to Survive When Your Ship is Sinking: Weathering Life's Storms*

**CONTACT:**

Allison Daniels Ministries, LLC

P. O. Box 1571

Clinton, Maryland 20735

(202) 258-4987

Email: AllisonGDaniels@verizon.net

Website: www.AllisonGDaniels.com

Blog: http://lifegoeson-allisongdaniels.blogspot.com

YouTube: AGDaniels29

www.ingramcontent.com/pod-product-compliance
Lightning Source LLC
Chambersburg PA
CBHW071542080526
44588CB00011B/1752